Startled by Music
new poetry in traditional forms

FEATURING

BILL CUSHING

edited by Laura Vosika

Gabriel's Horn Publishing

Copyright 2024 by Laura Vosika and Gabriel's Horn Press

All rights reserved. No portion of this book may be reproduced, stored in any retrieval system, or transmitted in any form or by any means electronic, mechanical, photocopy, recording, scanning, or other except for brief quotations in reviews or articles, without the prior written permission of the author and publisher.

Cover Design: Laura Vosika

Contact editors@gabrielshornpress.com

Published in the United States by Gabriel's Horn Press

First printing 2024 in the United States
For sales, visit www.gabrielshornpress.com
PRINT ISBN: 979-8-88846-088-7

Other Books by Gabriel's Horn

The Blue Bells Chronicles: a tale of time travel….
- *Blue Bells of Scotland*
- *The Minstrel Boy*
- *The Water is Wide*
- *Westering Home*
- *The Battle is O'er*

Food and Feast in the World of the Blue Bells Chronicles: a gastronomic historic poetic musical romp in thyme

The Space Between trilogy, Shawn D. Brink

My Gypsy War Diary, Shawn D. Brink

Gabriel's Horn Poetry Anthologies
- Startled by JOY: 2019
- Startled by NATURE: 2020
- Startled by LOVE: 2021
- Startled by HUMOR: 2022

A Dream of Dragons, Laurie Kehoe

A Woman of Many Names, Ilona Miler

The Feet Say Run, Dan Blum

Gypsy Heart, Lily Gelle

The Path that Shines: a story of life, love, and loss, Dr. Chris R. Powell

Shattered Faith, Rebecca May Hope

Silken Strands, Rebecca May Hope

Destination Harmony, Rebecca May Hope

…and many more

STARTLED BY MUSIC

featuring

BILL CUSHING

STARTLED BY MUSIC

Love	1
Humor	7
Nature's Music	15
Music in Daily Life	25
Famous Musicians	35
Musicians	45
Music and Faith	57
Music's Healing Power	65
Instruments	71
Poetry Forms	77
Poets' Bios	81
Afterword	92

LOVE

Music and Beauty

Part I: The Maiden's Melody

In the quiet of the night, a song is born,
A dulcet tune that through the air is torn.
Like a maiden fair with henna hair so bright,
Her voice, a melody that takes its flight.

Part II: The Locket's Love

A locket clasped, within it love does dwell,
A secret kept, a story to foretell.
As music flows, so does her heart's refrain,
A symphony of love, in joy and pain.

Part III: The Harmony of Souls

Together they dance, the song and the maid,
In harmony, their beauty never fades.
For music is the locket's gentle clasp,
Uniting hearts in an eternal grasp.

— C. R. Powell

Three part Italian sonnet

Poem for a Love Song

In the night, the song waves start to disappear
Like white trees, when there's no one a fall to hear.
Earth's shadow hides the moon, a harp without strings.
Lasting love shines on crazy engagement rings.

What does love mean when the elves come to life cheer?
In the night, the song waves start to disappear,
And in the moonlight, your feelings become blue.
The flowers cry for our time with tears of dew.

Bud butterflies become whispers in our dreams
To complete our blue entwining in life's streams.
In the night, the song waves start to disappear
On the moon, a double-meaning pamphleteer.

The green knows that through the darkness shines the light.
Love has a sense when the saints pray for the height.
And life blooms when the Lord's angels hurry near.
In the night, the song waves start to disappear.

— Marieta Maglas

Quatern

Composed over a lifetime

Every note has been written for you.
It is free-flowing, and it is gushing.
Come, my love, let us have an impromptu
Rehearsal; it'll begin by just humming.
All my feelings are wrapped up in it.
My heart and soul are contained.
I can't pretend I haven't been tortured over it.
Here I've nothing left out or restrained.
I hand over to you, this music sheet.
Composed over a whole lifetime
Just so you can hear it's no ragtime,
It's no blues; yes, it's bittersweet.
Come, please listen. Sit on this loveseat.
Even my heart has a metronome beat.

— Mark Heathcote

Alternate rhyming stanzas

I see your breath

I see your breath
in the candle's flame
dancing to night's music

— Jennifer Gurney

Haiku

Homecoming

To a parent or a child
there is no sweeter music
the humming of a song
being held near to another's heart
There is no sweeter music
whatever age one may be
being held near to another's heart
every touch a symphony
Whatever age one may be
to know you're welcomed home
every touch a symphony
to a parent or a child.

— deb y. felio

Pantoum

Humor

The Kazoo's Cry

In halls of sound where silence once did reign,
A kazoos' cry now breaks the solemn chain.
With honks and toots, they claim their rightful place,
In symphonies, they find their merry grace.

The maestro frowns, his baton drops with dread,
As kazoos blare, the orchestra's bled.
Yet in this chaos, joy does find its way,
For music's heart beats strong in every day.

So let us laugh at kazoos' bold display,
Their brassy voices lead us on our way.
In every note, a story to be told,
Of kazoos brave and music's magic hold.

— C. R. Powell

iambic pentameter

Between Sets: Scene from a Film Noir

After jazzing to a pianola,
"I am," says Lola-Lola,
sucking a finger
of rum in flat co-cola,
"not just a girl singer
but a humdinger,

so be my, be my heart's volcano,
my body's hard tornado"—
her sloe eyes tearing
as if she could be made to
prefer his half-soused leering
to the diamond earrings,

the crystal pom-poms
sparkling on his sweaty palm.
Though hot ice scalds,
she reaches wide-eyed for them,
willing to risk a fall
for brilliants, even if flawed.

— J.S. Absher

Form: aababb.

Music Therapy

Hippety, hoppity,
Simon and Garfunkel
Offer a therapy
Better than talk:
After I listen to
"Kodachrome," "Julio"
Ritualistically,
"I am a Rock."

— Rebecca May Hope

Double Dactyl

Bassoona

A man from Altoona
Played a maple bassoona
He played it so loud
He scared off the crowd
As if they were fleeing a typhoona

— Roberta Sachs

Limerick

Clarinet

A young poet played clarinet
All the while she couldn't forget:
She'd tried for a time
But she still couldn't find
A rhyme for the composer Bizet

— Roberta Sachs

Limerick

Poet's Note:
For those who don't know, Bizet is pronounced bi-Zay.
For those who do know, this is the joke of the poem. She's trying to rhyme the wrong thing.

Confidentiality

Hi-de-ho, ho-de-ho,
Poor Mrs. Robinson
Has no more privacy,
Threatens to sue:
Pharmacological
Problems fall under the
Purview of HIPAA now—
Coo-coo-ca-choo!

— Rebecca May Hope

Double Dactyl

Trombone

A man of New Ulm played trombone
While riding a stately young roan
The horse shook its ear
And suddenly reared
It seemed it preferred baritone!

— Roberta Sachs

Limerick

English Horn, Cor Anglaise

My true love sweetly played the cor anglaise
Although I argued 'twas the English horn
And yet her lilting sounds I did embrace
Drifting, ethereal melodies so forlorn
If only because they seared the aching ear
With dreadful honk that earnestly sought for grace
Of delicate flute; but only brought a tear
To eye and unwilled grimace to the face

Why could she not have played the lute or harp
A lovely sound so easy to embrace?
But chose instead the sounds of dying carp
That purse her lips and twist her lovely face?

And though it's more than ever should be born
Because I love her, I love her English horn

— Roberta Sachs

English Sonnet

Wreck

Gitchigoo, Gotchagoo,
Edmund Fitzgerald song
Eerily haunts me and
Sticks in my brain;
Musicologically
Lightfoot advises me:
"Going to Michigan?
Travel by train!"

— Rebecca May Hope

Double Dactyl

Nature's Music

The Lilting Refrain of the Irish Sea

The sea's green-blue whisper, *a súil agus* song,
Grain dances to the tune of the eternal sea.
In the wind's caress, *na gréine síol* is strong.

The waves' soft murmur, *a fáinne's* gentle throng,
Harmonizes with the grain's wild spree.
The sea's green-blue whisper, *a súil agus* song.

Na gréine síol, in the breeze they belong,
A melody of life, forever free.
In the wind's caress, *na gréine síol* is strong.

The horizon's call, where sky and sea prolong,
A symphony of nature, for all to see.
The sea's green-blue whisper, *a súil agus* song.

Na gréine síol, in the wind they throng,
A dance of existence, wild and free.
In the wind's caress, *na gréine síol* is strong.

So let us listen to the sea's sweet prolong,
Its green-blue lilt, a gift from the sea.
The sea's green-blue whisper, *a súil agus* song,
In the wind's caress, *na gréine síol* is strong.

[*na gréine síol*: seed of the sun
a súil agus: from the eye]

— C. R. Powell

Villanelle

Thunderstorm

front porch
rowdy thunderstorm
summer music

— Jennifer Gurney

Haiku

Pantoum for the Summer Dance

The rainbow ribbons still stretching in the blue rain
Are like snakes waking up at the tune of the jazz flutes.
Butterflies chase bumble bees singing duets in vain.
Summer dances around some red roses and green fruits.

When the snakes wake up at the tune of the jazz flutes,
Summer slips over the meadow her dream of green.
She dances around some red roses and green fruits.
The moon rises from the cloud's fence like a queen.

Summer slips over the meadow like a dream of green
In a fall sky having puffy winds and a dim light.
The moon rises from the cloud's fence like a queen.
With green shadows, the sprites appear all around the sight.

The fall sky has puffs of clouds and a floating light.
Butterflies chase bumble bees singing duets in vain.
With green shadows, the sprites appear all around the sight.
Summer rainbow's ribbon still stretches in the blue rain.

— Marieta Maglas

Pantoum

Atonal Music in a Rondeau

A deliberate wind from the dark side
of distant moons comes to earth on neap tide,
travels through ozone holes, from mountain tops
to gorges deep, across the Steppes, no stops,
through Gobi Desert, tundra, glaciers, can't hide.
Its path of whispers, groans, curses is wide,
gusts through evening trees on the inside,
then dangling from shaking branches, it hops.
A deliberate wind from the dark side.
I wear my cloak of warm comfort outside,
sins all washed away with joy for the ride.
Hear noble notes, melodies from treetops
where angelic music rebalances, swaps
atonal sounds with a harmonic glide.
A deliberate wind, now bonafide.

— Evie Groch

Rondeau

Nature

Nature
resounds her song
in stillness and in breeze
chickadees and cicadas sing
Listen!

— deb y felio

Cinquain

Uguisu

While walking from Yamashina over
hills with bamboo to Kyoto I heard a
liquid loveliness of a bird of a
quality to pause me in step to spur
my poised attention should the song recur
as the *precipitous quaver* was a
touch of *ethereal elegance* a
reminder of innocence and wonder
that I could be in a moment taken
from the circular nature of my thought
and transfixed to listen to hear once more
that sound as an *impetus to waken*
from nets of opinion that had me caught
to an eerie dimension I adore.

— Tekkan

Italian sonnet

Blossom Symphony

Blossoms unfurl —
a single phrase repeated
over and over —
orchards heartbeat.

A single phrase repeated,
embellished by a bumble bee —
orchards heart beat
where leaf veins breathe.

Embellished by a bumble bee
and fortissimo nightjar churr —
leaf veins breathe
and voles chomp on June-drop litter.

Fortissimo nightjar churr —
counter melody from wasps.
voles chomp on June-drop litter —
wing-purr of hawk-moths.

Counter melody from wasps
and woodpecker drumrolls,
wing-purr of hawk-moths,
and mineral-water arpeggios.

Woodpecker drumrolls
whilst sky rests in roots.
Mineral-water arpeggios
swell embryo fruits.

Sky rests in roots
liquid sun rushes through branches —
swells embryo fruits.
Under trees they clink glasses.

Liquid sun gushes through branches
they listen to the bubble fizz.
Under trees they clink glasses —
share a cider kiss.

They listen to the bubble fizz
over and over —
share a cider kiss
as blossoms unfurl.

— Diana Sanders

Pantoum

Music in Daily Life

The Best Set

During my Classic Celtic music shows
I play some songs that everyone knows
Their souls are stirred with "Oh Danny Boy"
While the light-hearted reels are full of joy.

I practice daily all my songs
Perfecting my technique from any wrongs
When at the piano I begin
My spirit soars and then I grin.

For it doesn't matter what I play
I know what all the folks will say
They love to meet a friendly songbird
Who plays the music they have heard.

But there's one set they like the best
And time has shown it's not in jest
The "Turkey In The Straw" most certainly comes first
Which makes their gentle hearts soon burst.

Then "The Irish Washerwoman" jig
Is something that they really truly dig
For the simple early American tune
With this Irish ditty makes them swoon!

— Luisa Reyes

Rhymed Couplets

Cleaning

>my best cleaning--
>to loud rock music and the
>pressure of company
>
>— Jennifer Gurney
>
>*Haiku*

Charm

>name charm clinking
>against her water bowl
>music
>
>— Jennifer Gurney
>
>*Haiku*

At the Graves of Those Who Made Me Sing

They had quick tongues, hot tempers.
The room shook when they walked.
And I—timid and tongue-
tied when they talked

praising my shy smile, my teeth
(amazed I ate potatoes
raw), and lauding my sweet
unbroken soprano—

I call them out: Elbert not forgotten,
his wife, much put upon,
and loving mother Emma.
They led me on

into a room of their country store,
through the Sunday prattle
of men joking and swapping
lies and cattle.

"Hide if you like in this cardboard box,"
they said, "but sing out loud
and clear." Who was it threw
the copper cloud

of Lincoln pennies that rained down
and clattered inside the box
like the pinions in a shaken
pendulum clock?

Time took those who made me sing
and tucked them under grass
and told them, You have nothing
to give or ask

till called upon. White-tailed deer
will leap the fence to graze
between your headstones scrawled
with lichen and praise.

— J.S. Absher

Form: An invented form. The second and fourth line in each stanza rhyme; the first line is tetrameter; the next two lines are trimeter, and the last is dimeter, except for the final line of the poem, a trimeter.

Publication credit: J.S. Absher, *Mouth Work* (St Andrews University Press, 2016)

Ode to Reiko, Our Hostess

A Japanese house in Kanazawa awaits us.
Shoes parked inside the door, slippers hungry for feet.
Tatami mats caress the floors like lace on armchair backs.
They invite us in, to step on them; we softly tread into your
home amid bows, smiles, doozos to find a Shinto shrine
and another to Buddha you point out to us.
Family in frames on walls betrays your humble pride –
a grandson Kendo master in full regalia.
You bow again, make us tea served with cubes
of sweet anko paste. You model how to cut with the
mini-spear on our saucers. We watch and do.
We're doozo-ed into an outer room as you kneel
near your koto to sing and play for us a haunting melody;
voice and strings marry in soft deliberation. We absorb
the notes with ears open and eyes closed. It ends too soon.
We ask for more. You modestly consent.

We're no longer from America or from anywhere but Japan,
letting the music carry us away from ourselves, across borders
never before reached, to a space of awe and insight.
The suggestion of walls speak to the impermanent nature
of our experience. Rooms are multi-purposed, engaging
all loving activities of life. We picture your children being
raised here, the sleeping quarters cleverly camouflaged
for ulterior uses.
Your nine words of English, our eight words of Japanese
are enough to bridge our cultures in a house of welcome.
As we return our feet to our American shoes, we wonder
how long your Kanazawa spirit will linger inside us.

— Evie Groch

Ode

Ode to Flamenco

A dance is a dance
but you, Flamenco, are spirit in flame.
Your arched spine of strength
spreads shivers to stomping feet,
to fingers that caress castanets,
pulse out codes that hypnotize
with staccato rhythms
yet preserve a delicate beckoning
to engage in a rendezvous.
Petticoats of white foam
accent the illusive hem of a
dress sewn to entice the romance
out of the underground and into which
a body is poured ounce by ounce
to move to the wails and claps
of the *cante flamenco.*
A *pericón* behind which to hide her face,
a *peineta* to crown her head,
an unchained force that claims the stage.
A dance is a dance
But, you, Flamenco, are raw, unrobed romance.

— Evie Groch

Ode

A Magical Moment

He took the stage to share some spoken word.
He started in, the crowd was feeling right.
We recognized the lines as ones we'd heard,
Instead of poetry, he did recite
The lyrics to an old Bon Jovi song.
Soon everyone began to sing along
In joyfully united vocal throng,
A moment that was perfectly absurd.
We all released our hidden inner nerd
With volume and with passion at its height,
A sense of joined community was stirred
That made life almost magical that night.
We finished with a flourish, loud and strong,
And held the final note out way too long,
But nothing we might do now could be wrong.
Contentment flowed, the whole room simply purred.

— Jerri Hardesty

Lyrical Ballad

Streaming Music

After Aunt Hazel sang A Wee Little Man and Itsy Bitsy Spider
After Daddy played Patsy and Hank on the stereo,
After kindergarten Bright Coral Bells, Kookaburra Sits in the Old Gum Tree,
After Panes Angelicus and Queen of the May in the school choir,
After Johnny Fedora in the spring concert,
After I Want to Hold Your Hand on Ed Sullivan,
After Chim Chim Che-ree in the talent show,
After Sam Was a Man and It was a Lover and his Lass at the festival,
After Now is the Month of Maying and April is my Mistress Face a cappella,
After Leaving on a Jet Plane acoustic guitar in hand,
After White Bird, Both Sides Now, Go Ask Alice, female vocalists,
After harmonies with the car radio, especially, CSNY,
After bluegrass fests and Appalachian folk tunes,
After all the music in my head, singing in the shower,
After all, this is what I want.
After all is said and done, lyrics, melodies, sound tracks, exaltation.

— Donna Isaac

anaphoric litany

Famous Musicians

To a Stadium Where Pink Floyd Performed

Fifty thousand seats within those walls
Not one for me – no ticket, no cash to pay
The concert of a lifetime to me calls
In Arrowhead Stadium where the Chiefs play
But football will not take the field tonight
No tailgate grills, no last chance scalper's deals
Just Pink Floyd, the greatest of all time
What I wouldn't give if I just might
Be inside that edifice to steal
A precious moment; it could be no crime

Standing in Missouri's summer heat
I wait and watch the lucky people climb
Concrete spiral ramps to find their seats
The worst of sections, I'd consider prime
Imagining the shadow o' buttressed wall
Imposing nightfall on the crowded yard
The laser lights illuminating clouds
David Gilmour, Mason, Wright and all
The echoing opening notes hit me hard
And the roaring of the passionate crowd

O'er the walls the chords and lyrics fly
For melancholy hours as I stand
Below your towering rampart in the sky
Hearkening this most amazing band
Then as they finish with "Comfortably Numb"
A stylish couple comes strolling through the gate
The man holds up his ticket stub to me
'Can this be real?' I thought and stood there dumb
Then sallied past the guard and not too late
For the finest encore I might ever see

I hear and feel "Hey You" and "Run Like Hell"
Three-D effects, the audience, the band
For now I'm part of the Division Bell
At the tunnel entrance where I stand
Arrowhead, you played your role so well
The greatest venue, say I, across the land

— Danny Fantod

Ode

Imayo For Diana Schurr

Her body waxes and wanes like the moon, but her honeyed voice
remains true, mercurial in range, constant in sustain.
The world, living within her, sounds of beauty without sight.

— Bill Cushing

Imayo

Mozart

Mozart fills the air
With musical brilliance from
Centuries ago

— Jennifer Gurney

Haiku

Three Haiku for Heinrich Schütz

What small time is left
I spend in the company
Of the insolent:

Two sopranos, two
Tenors, two basses, and I,
The lone low-voiced girl.

All the city's syllables
Can't contain you,
My dear electric sun.

— C.M. Gigliotti

Haiku

Hiromi's Imayo

Playing like a mad hatter, Hiromi performs
glissando from Bach to blues, connects then to now.
Her face flaunts infectious fun—reflected in chords
through the music in her bones, transferred to the keys.

— Bill Cushing

Imayo

Hiromi is a Japanese jazz and classical pianist.

Ode to Otyken

They named themselves for the middle ground,
a place to meet, to lay weapons aside.
The pulse of a passing native sound
uses tarab to start the tide
in a surge of Siberian blood.
A man's graveled throat cause a cascade
as jazz melds tradition. In contrast,
drumming or hitting strings then flood
the swelling lilt of sirens' serenade
that bonds now to a mysterious tribal past.

— Bill Cushing

Ode

The Redbone Pantoum

Leon decked out in black, Ray-Bans perched on
a Syrid nose, his drooping moustache surrounds
the soul patch: a musical sage
peering from beneath that Panama hat.
Leon fretted multi-tonal sounds
from each and every timeless tune
with a voice sometimes smooth, then scat,
while coaxing that acoustic guitar.
Leon, ageless as a harvest moon,
did not die so much as exit the stage,
returning to the Araby bazaar,
and though gone, he continues to shine on.

— Bill Cushing

Pantoum

Kyrielle Sonnet for George Sand and Frédéric Chopin

Searching for their love ideal
To plant there a dawn so real,
God gave them hope to go ahead
And palm flowers for their dream bed.

In their naked room without windows,
Not touched by the innuendos,
Music was their way to be wed
And palm flowers had their dream bed,

The cradle of their nascent thought
Could cut their main Gordian knot-
Baptism of freedom in the head.
And palm flowers had their dream bed.

Searching for their love ideal
And palm flowers for their dream bed.

— Marieta Maglas

Sonnet

Musicians

Casual Muse

We walk around a corner to a square,
A grassy space with ancient looming trees.
We see him sitting, cross-legged, silent, there,
An old guitar at rest atop his knees.
He closes eyes and takes it in his hands,
And gently strokes the strings beneath his thumb.
A simple sound spills forth and then expands
Into a resonant harmonic hum.
And then, in earnest, he begins to play,
The fragile notes, so gossamer, so light,
Reminding me of flowers wild in May,
Or twinkling stars that frolic in the night.
Sometimes the unexpected circumstance
Inspires perfect chance for thoughts to dance.

— Jerri Hardesty

Shakespearean Sonnet

Imayo for the Soloist

Fluid fingers sprint across, sharing her love of
Tchaikovsky's concerto and, throwing her hair back,
untethers joy's energy. Even in tacit,
we listeners sit, in awe, enthusiastic.

— Bill Cushing

Imayo

Jesse

He practices each day on his guitar,
His dearest friend, his most delightful thing.
He does not even want to be a star,
He'd rather just write songs for kids to sing.
He teaches children lessons with no fee
To help them breathe the life into their art,
His funny lyrics make them squeal with glee.
Their laughter fills the void within his heart.
He grew up as an orphan, raised by nuns,
So now he spends his time and skills to grow
The love of music in these younger ones
To show them something beautiful to know.
He freely offers pieces of his soul,
The more he gives, the more it makes him whole.

— Jerri Hardesty

Shakespearean Sonnet

The Trashcan Man

He drives into the urban city streets,
His vehicle a rainbow-colored van.
He stops beside a park with benchlike seats,
And there unloads a metal garbage can.
He also has some buckets and some bowls,
Some milk jugs, sticks, and jars with beads of clay,
And with a single motion then he rolls
The trashcan upside down and starts to play.
He beats a simple rhythm, siren song,
And all the local children run to come.
They try the objects out, no sound is wrong,
Soon everyone is joining in to drum.
They say this neighborhood is dying, dead.
Today we're making music here instead.

— Jerri Hardesty

Shakespearean Sonnet

Jobe the One Man Band

With classic rock on the radio
In his twelve-foot custom van
He knows the words to every song
Jobe the one man band

Founders' days and festivals
From Houston to Saint Paul
Church bazaars and county fairs
He's glad to play them all

He pulls in town long after dark
But he knows where to go
He finds his spot and gets some rest
Before the early show

Morning dawns he tunes his Gretsch
Takes honey for his throat
He braces his harmonica
And dons his patchwork coat

The van's side panel rises up
He pounds the ivory keys
Keeping time on his kick drum
Cymbals between his knees

Singing "Let the Good Times Roll"
And "Me and Bobby McGee"
He gets the crowd to sing along
In or out of key

He has a horn and six-hole flute
A rack of bells and chimes
He'll play them all before he's done
Two, three at a time

He takes the time to talk about
The tales behind the songs
The guys and girls who made them great
When rock and roll was strong

Closing with the "Midnight Special"
He lets the van side down
Three more shows that afternoon
Then on to his next town

Before he hits the road that night
He walks up to the stage
To hear a band he used to love
Back in his younger days

"So hold on loosely, but don't let go…"
And he's sixteen again
Forming bands in dad's garage
With all his rowdy friends

With classic rock on the radio
He starts the custom van
And aims himself to his next show
Jobe the one man band

— Danny Fantod

Ballad

The Right Place at the Right Time

He sat upon a chair outside his door,
The dust of days gone by beneath his feet,
It was an old French Quarter music store
Along a lonely empty stretch of street.
He raised an old harmonica and blew
A note that echoed through the heat of June.
It grew into a song I thought I knew;
It was an old familiar Beatles' tune.
The way he played it, though, was all his own,
The phrasing rearranged to suit his style
That caused the melody to sway and moan
In ways that kept us lingering awhile.
He finished with a last harmonic slide,
Then tipped his hat, and disappeared inside.

— Jerri Hardesty

Shakespearean Sonnet

Electric

You're the rhythm maker—
cathartic screamer.
Out of shadow—
restless, animated

Cathartic screamer —
fingers, strings
restless, animated,
finely tuned.

Fingers, strings —
at one with drums
finely tuned
riding the crest.

At one with drums—
bass growls,
riding the crest
over pints and dogs.

Bass growls
through the crowd
over pints and dogs
into the fresh night.

Through the crowd
riffs squeeze
into the fresh night —
sorcerer in silhouette.

Riffs squeeze
out of shadow.
Sorcerer in silhouette —
You're the rhythm maker.

—Diana Sanders

Pantoum

Music

Your violin case is open, just as you left it.
I lift your violin and breathe
the smell of old wood, resin and a trace
of Interdit, your perfume of the moment.
I run my fingers over the wood —
touch the varnish where it has cracked.
That evening, I watched you release
the tension in your horsehair bow
before tucking it in.
The day having taken a glorious breath
of Fauré, Bach and Avro Pärt.
On good days when music came,
there was nothing else.
You were an acrobat of light.

— Diana Sanders

Sonnet

Music and Faith

Decibels of Praise

i. Now
The chorus of praise sung
by creation drowns out ours—
the white-throated sparrow
spilling its golden notes
on winter days; spring peepers
and katydids in their season.
In choosing to be human,
we yielded to sorrows that pierce
through hearts to joy. We chose
the flinty grace of arrows,
the grinding of the hours
that sharpens the callow young.
And when we want to cry
we sing a lullaby.

ii. Later
The first to rise will sing, Hallelujah!
and shake creation.
The sleeping will cry, What's that brouhaha?
while Christ calls out, My dears, I know you!
Such will be the exultation
when the first to rise sing, Hallelujah!
and shake creation.

iii. At Last
Thorny bougainvillea,
cells that move by cilia,
lichen and giraffe,
mother frog and bull calf,
the pampered and abused,
well-loved and ill-used
will see in their stories
the makings of glory
and join their sweet words
in praise of the Lord.

— J.S. Absher

Forms:

"Now"—Invented sonnet form: abcdef fedcba gg.
"Later"—triolet.
"At Last"—rhymed couplets

Publication credit: *Amethyst Review, August 2022*

The Whisper of the Muse

The whisper of the muse
With his violin bow in hand, the man plays,
then stops and listens to his whispering muse.
Where others were entranced, he breaks and weighs,
His face, solemn in thought, was much less enthused.
Resembling a wilting flower head, drooped
The world looks like a man. Who-has-been duped?
He's old, and he has passed this way before.
He knows off by heart the music in his soul-
has sealed inside, and like a green Hellebore
In the wintertime, his head will rise and roll.
And the blood of Christ, a clap of thunder
makes all bolt up straight in awe and wonder.

— Mark Heathcote

Sonnet

Christmas

Christmas
Pavarotti
Adeste fideles
Reverberates eternally
Sublime

— Jacqueline Anderson

Cinquain

Faith's Music

Faith is the music that lifts the soul
Let its rich harmonies give beauty to life
Let its melodies make you whole
Faith is the music that lifts the soul
With gratitude and joy beyond control
No matter the troubles or strife
Faith is the music that lifts the soul
Let its rich harmonies give beauty to life

— Christina Lincoln

Triolet

God, he's the greatest conductor of them all

God, he's the greatest conductor of them all
Johann Sebastian Bach, his-like-a-heavenly footnote
Wolfgang Amadeus Mozart, his-a-magical waterfall
Igor Stravinsky, a dawn chorus now about to be bulldozed
But God, he's the greatest conductor of them all
Gustavo Mahler, he's-a-dancing acrobatic butterfly,
Franz Joseph Haydn, he's a mountain-range-forest a fireball
Pyotr Ilyich Tchaikovsky, he's a flood, a starry sky to stupefy,
But God, he's the greatest conductor of them all
George Frideric Handel, he's like-sombre-moonlight happily reflected
Antonio Lucio Vivaldi, he's-heart-leaping enthrall.
George Gershwin is playfully romantic blood & tissue-connected
But God, he's the greatest conductor of them all
He's the one with the real musicality rapport
He's the one all these composers try to extoll.

— Mark Heathcote

Rhymes and refrain

Music's Healing Power

Crescendo

Driving down the street
Mind full of anxieties
Hearing music play
The orchestra's crescendo
Silences the noise within

— Jacqueline Anderson

Tanka

Unforgettable Ballad

Memories return
The ballad is remembered
Song engraved in heart

— Vanessa Caraveo

Haiku

Leaf in the Wind

Leaf in the wind
the sun is a touch
it's yellow and green
don't think about it much

wind is a force
an invisible push
a joy to hear
the melody is lush

trees are choirs
adoration for ears
a turbulence
counterbalance of fears

salvation here
a momentary flow
solace and peace
with the quiet I grow.

— Tekkan

Rhymed Quatrains

Music's Harmonies

Music's harmonies
Work in our bodies and souls
Miracle healing

— Annette Moore

Haiku

A Child's Song

The baby cries through the long night
so I will sing him a nursery rhyme so he can sleep well.
He enjoys the music with a smile so bright.
The baby cries through the long night
but music calms him, so he'll be alright.
He begins to get sleepy I am able to tell.
The baby cries through the long night
so I will sing him a nursery rhyme so he can sleep well.

— Vanessa Caraveo

Triolet

Instruments

Marvelous Instrument

Moved by the piano
Instrument touches my soul
A song of marvel

— Vanessa Caraveo

Haiku

Love Melody

Melody of love
The violin plays for her
Notes express feelings

— Vanessa Caraveo

Haiku

Irish harps

Irish harps cast a spell when played well.
It could be that those players are pretty.
And they put me under some, kind of spell.
Secretly, my heart wants to accompany:

Drum to every string, and hope one looks
From me, and they'll lose their heart, their key.
Oh, Irish Rose, you keep me on tenterhooks.
Oh, Irish harps cast a spell on me.

The hand that plucks this chord must grasp the flame.
And touch the burning that can't be doused.
And not even a good strong stout can drain
The way she picks those strings out of my heart

Irish harps cast a spell when played well.
Oh, Emerald Isle, you're the star of my heart.
Oh, look at me now, dumbstruck, open-mouthed.
It could be desire comes to me unannounced.

— Mark Heathcote

Rhyming stanzas

Give me a link between music and art

Give me a link between music and art-
a large canvas that in truth can impart
an oil brush, leap out of mirrored age's dark
something resonating with Mozart or Bach,

give me compositions charcoaled in kohl,
colours; burning feathery bright, like crests,
like a red-hot poker searing my soul,
wind and string instruments played in quartets.

Give me choirs in accord, the sound of harps.
Angels seated on nimbus clouds in arcs-
eyeing a pianist in reverence,
playing scores of songs in exuberance;

evoking flames and flowers dying daily,
dreams as heady as a mare dancing gaily
over a valley, the mountain waters,
notes ♪ and brushes—are swimming sea otters.

I want real music that thunders and rains,
not just cherry blossoms drifting down lanes.
I want art that strains to be heard-not-seen,
blended swapped over, only to reconvene.

— Mark Heathcote

Rhyming stanzas followed by couplet quatrains

Saxophone

When twilight whispers through the evening air,
A saxophone begins its serenade,
Its melodies that gently swell and flair,
In moonlit shadows a figure softly played.

Oh saxophone, you call us to the night,
Where love and longing smoothly interlace.
Your soulful voice, so mellow and so right,
In every breath, I feel sweet love's embrace.

Echoes fade, yet linger on the breeze,
A waltz of memories in the sleepy mind.
The solo glides and weaves through ancient trees,
Among the swaying branches, love defined.
The player glides away and no one sees
He's left a melody of love behind

— J.A. Sellers

Sonnet

POETRY FORMS

Anaphoric Litany

Anaphora is a poetic device in which lines begin with the same repeated words or phrase.

Ballad

A ballad typically is a story told in stanzas of four lines with the second and fourth lines rhyming.

Cinquain

5 lines, similar to haiku and tanka.
Lines 1 and 5 have 2 syllables.
Lines 2, 3, and 4 have more syllables, giving them a diamond shape.
They should tell a small story with action, feeling, and a conclusion.

Double Dactyl

A dactyl is a foot in poetry which consists of a long syllable followed by two short syllables.
2 stanzas, each with three lines of dactyl dimeter followed by a line of choriamb (long short short long)
The last lines of the two stanzas must rhyme.
The first line of the first stanza is repetitive nonsense.
The second line of the first stanza is the subject of the poem.
At least one line must be entirely one double-dactyl word.

Haiku

3 lines of 5 syllables, 7 syllables, 5 syllables.

Imayo

A Japanese poem of 4 lines with 12 syllables per line. There is a 'pause' after the 7th syllable of each line. It was originally written to be sung.

Limerick

Limericks are typically humorous. They have five lines with the rhyme scheme AABBA. A lines have 7-10 syllables while B lines have 5-7 syllables.

Ode

Odes are typically poems of praise. It should be solemn and serious in tone. It should have uniform metrical feet but this is often not strictly observed. Traditional odes include Pindar, Horatian, and irregular.

Pantoum

A series of quatrains of ABAB, in which the second rhyme (B) becomes the first rhyme of the next quatrain. So ABAB BCBC CDCD DEDE etc.

Rondeau

A 13-line poem divided into stanzas of 5, 3, and 5 lines with only two rhymes throughout. The opening words of the first line become a refrain at the end of the second and third stanzas.

Sonnet

Sonnets are 14 lines, traditionally 8 lines and then 6. They typically use iambic pentameter and a rhyme scheme. There are several variations on the sonnet:

Italian, or Petrarchan: rhyme scheme of ABBA ABBA followed by either CDEDCE or CDCDCD.

English, Shakespearean, or Elizabethan: rhyme scheme AB AB CDCD EFEF GG

In a sonnet, the first 8 lines typically propose a problem or ask a question. The question is answered in the last 6 lines.

Tanka

A Japanese poem of five lines. The first and third have five syllables; the second, fourth, and fifth have seven syllables. It should give a complete picture of an event or mood.

Quatern

Four stanzas of four lines each. Line 1 of Stanza 1 recurs on line 2 or stanza 2, line 3 of stanza 3 and line 4 of stanza 4.

Triolet

The triolet has 8 lines, usually of 8 syllables each. Rhyme scheme ABaAabAB. Thus, the first, fourth, and seventh lines are identical. The second and eighth lines are identical. The third, fifth, and sixth lines rhyme with either A or B.

Villanelle

19 lines; five tercets (three-line stanzas) of ABA with a quatrain (four lines) at the end with ABAA. The first and third lines of the first tercet alternate as the final lines of the following tercets and form the last two lines of the last quatrain.

POET BIOS

FEATURED POET

BILL CUSHING

Born into a Navy family, Bill Cushing lived in several states as well as the Virgin Islands and Puerto Rico before moving to California where he still resides with his wife and their son. Because of his experience in the Navy and later as a marine electrician prior to beginning studies at the University of Central Florida, classmates dubbed him the "blue collar poet."

Bill earned an MFA in writing from Goddard College in Vermont and taught in Los Angeles area colleges for more than 20 years.

Bill has four poetry collections: *A Former Life* (awarded a Kops-Fetherling International Book Award), *Music Speaks* (winner of the 2019 San Gabriel Valley Poetry Festival chapbook award and a 2021 New York City Book Award), a chapbook incorporating a number of ekphrastic poems, and most recently *Just A Little Cage of Bone*.

Bill's work has been published in print and online by a variety of magazines, journals, and anthologies. Bill was honored as one of the Top Ten L. A. Poets in 2017, was named one of the "poets to watch" in 2018, and has previously had work nominated for a Pushcart Prize and Best of the Net. His "Sonnet to Slaughter" won the Helen Schaible Annual Sonnet Award, and "Cusqueños" was honored by Four Feathers Press in its category of poems about other countries.

Besides his poetry books, he has a collection of short stories (*The Commies Come to Waterton*) and a book of personal narratives (*Time Well Spent*).

His most recent book, *Heroic Brothers of the Civil War,* won a 2023 Global Literary Award for historical non-fiction.

Bill also performs with an area musician in a collaboration they have named Notes and Letters.

ALL POETS

J.S. Absher

J.S. Absher (www.jsabsherpoetry.com/) has published two full-length books of poetry, *Skating Rough Ground* (Kelsay Press, 2022) and *Mouth Work* (St. Andrews University Press), winner of the 2015 Lena Shull Award from the NC Poetry Society. Absher's poems have been published or accepted in dozens of publications. He lives in Raleigh, NC, with his wife, Patti. He is the featured poet for the 2024 Gabriel's Horn Poetry Anthology *Startled by FAITH 2024*.

Jaqueline Anderson

Jackie lives on the Texas gulf coast. Her work has been published in many anthologies. She enjoys traveling with her husband, visiting with her grandchildren & cooking vegan foods. She loves short form poetry and hopes to publish her own collection of poems in the near future.

Vanessa Caraveo

Vanessa Caraveo is an award-winning bilingual author, published poet, and artist who has a passion for promoting inclusion, empowerment and equality for all, helping others discover the power they possess within themselves to overcome adversity and persevere in life. Her work brings focus to many social issues that exist in today's world and has been published in *Literature Today Journal, Poetrybay, The Raven Review, Anacua Literary Arts Journal,* and for various anthologies throughout the years.

Danny Fantod

Danny Fantod, also known as Daniel Singer, is an aspiring author from Kansas, USA. He studied English at the Wichita State University and attended Johnson County Community College in Olathe, Kansas. His wife Beth, an avid reader and veteran educator, helps Danny with story ideas, first reads, and editorial advice.

"I've always had an ambition to write something meaningful, to tell stories that people are glad to read. After much procrastination and many false starts I am sharing with the world. The time has come to give voice to a lifetime of thoughts and memories."

Deb Y. Felio

deb y felio, in Boulder CO writes late at night on the mundane and the miraculous in all of life. Her work is published online and in print, including anthologies: Hay(na)ku 15; Minnie's Diary, A Southern Literary Review October (2018) ;and Gabriel's Horn:Startled by Joy and Startled by Nature (2020), Refuse to Stay Silent (2020) commemorating the centennial of the 19th amendment , I-70 Review, 2022. Her acrostic was published in How to Write a Form Poem by Tania Runyan, and her untitled cherita sequence was a finalist in the MacQueens's Quarterly March 2021 ekphrastic challenge.

C.M. Gigliotti

C.M. Gigliotti is a multi-hyphenate artist with degrees from Central Connecticut State University and the Writers Institute at Susquehanna University. Her poetry appears in *CommuterLit, The Twin Bill, Rough Cut Press, MEMEZINE, Songs of Eretz, Prose*

Poems, and elsewhere. She also writes on Substack at *Così faccio io*. She has lived in Germany since 2019.

Evie Groch

Evie Groch's opinion pieces, humor, poems, short stories, and recipes have been published in the New York Times, The SF Chronicle, The Contra Costa Times, The Journal, Games Magazine, in various anthologies and online. Her themes are travel, languages, immigration and justice of which she writes in *Half the Hurricanes*.

Jennifer Gurney

Jennifer Gurney lives in Colorado where she teaches, paints, writes and hikes. Her poetry has appeared internationally in a wide variety of journals, two of her poems have won international contests and one was recently turned into a choral piece for a concert. Jennifer's first book of poetry, *My Eyes Adjusting*, has recently been published.

Jerri Hardesty

Jerri Hardesty lives in the woods of Alabama with husband, Kirk, also a writer. They run the nonprofit poetry organization, New Dawn Unlimited, Inc. (NewDawnUnlimited.com)

Jerri has had over 700 poems published and has won more than 2400 awards and titles in both written and spoken word/performance poetry.

Rebecca May Hope

Rebecca May Hope teaches writing at a homeschool academy and a liberal arts university. Her longer works include two historical fiction novels and an award-winning contemporary Christian novella. Her short works—memoirs and short stories—have been published in anthologies and online literary magazines. She lives in Champlin, Minnesota, with her husband, who is also an author.

Mark Heathcote

Mark Andrew Heathcote is an adult learning difficulties support worker. He has poems published in journals, magazines, and anthologies online and in print. He resides in the UK and is from Manchester. Mark is the author of "In Perpetuity" and "Back on Earth," two books of poems published by Creative Talents Unleashed.

Donna Isaac

Donna is a teaching artist and organizer of community readings and workshops through the League of Minnesota Poets. Her published work includes *Footfalls* (Pocahontas Press); *Tommy* (Red Dragonfly Press); *Holy Comforter* (Red Bird Chapbooks); and *Persistence of Vision* (Finishing Line Press). Her work has also appeared in journals. She misses the Blue Ridge Mountains and warmer climes of the southern states but enjoys living on a pond a la Thoreau with its wildlife and seasonal wonders.

Christina Lincoln

Christina is a poet and writer. Her greatest love is her family—her husband, six children, and two mastiffs. With several children raised and out in the world, she now devotes more time to writing, poetry, and gardening. A native of the coast of Maine, Christina is a great lover of any and all seafood—especially with white wine.

Marieta Maglas

Marieta has been published in The MockingOwl Roost, Lothlorien Journal, Verse-Virtual, Silver Birch Press, Sybaritic Press, Kingfisher Poetry, Oddville Press, Prolific Press, Dashboard Horus, Coin-Operated Press, Mayari Literature, Synchronized Chaos, Al-Khemia Poetica, PentaCat Press, The Queer Gaze, Phoenix Z Publishing, All Your Poems Magazine, Ellerslie Books, Journal of the Akita International Haiku Network, Tuck Magazine, Southern Arizona Press, Republic Magazine, Ardus Publications, and others.

Annette Moore

Annette is a native of Virginia, currently living in New England where she loves to garden and visit the ocean, both of which are favorite subjects of her writing. After many years in business, she began writing in 2016. She loves poetry for its ability to speak great truths and wisdom succinctly and in unique ways.

C.R. Powell

Dr. Powell is an author, poet, musician, engineering and management consultant and aspiring polymath with his fingers on everything from fretboards and ivories to the pulse of post-modernism, surrealism, and nihilism's impact on morality and sanity. His work takes him from supercomputers to AI. In his spare time, he's an inventor.

Luisa Reyes

Luisa Kay Reyes' essay, "Thank You", is the winner of the April 2017 memoir contest of "The Dead Mule School Of Southern Literature". Her Christmas poem was a first place winner in the 16th Annual Stark County District Library Poetry Contest. Additionally, her essay "My Border Crossing" received a Pushcart Prize nomination from the Port Yonder Press. And two of her essays have been nominated for the "Best of the Net" anthology. With one of her essays recently being featured on "The Dirty Spoon" radio hour.

Roberta Sachs

In the hours after her day job as a veterinarian, Roberta likes to relax with a glass of red wine and a book of poetry. While a fan of Keats and Yeats, or Kates and Yates as she likes to call them, she finds herself drawn to writing more humorous observatioins drawn from her love of animals and the natural world.

Diana Sanders

Diana Sanders is a musician, composer and poet who lives in North Wales. Much of her inspiration comes from music and the amazing landscape in which she lives. She has had music and poetry published in the UK, USA and India.

J.A. Sellers

After growing up on a farm in Nebraska, J.A. Sellers earned degrees in philosophy and English, which led, through unexpected twists and turns, to a career in finance and banking, which led to the opportunity to travel, particularly to Eastern Europe and Asia, to study many cultures, and return finally to writing and poetry. J.A. Sellers is currently working on a first book of poetry.

Tekkan

Barry MacDonald goes by the *dharma* name "*Tekkan*," which means "Iron Man" in 13th century Japanese. *Tekkan* indicates a "settled practitioner of great determination." He was given this name when he took Buddhist vows.

Tekkan was the featured poet in the 2022 volume of *Startled by Laughter* and was in the top ten of 2,000 poets published by the first issue of *Maplestaple* in a literary contest in 2023. He has also been published in numerous publications.

Editor

Laura Vosika

Laura Vosika is the author of *The Blue Bells Chronicles,* a tale of time travel, action and adventure, romance and redemption, across modern and medieval Scotland.

She has had poetry published in *The Mocassin* and *Martin Lake Journal.* Her first collection of music has been released under the name *Glenmirril Garden.* She co-hosts *Books and Brews with Laura Vosika and Chris Powell,* which interviews authors and poets while pairing their work to beer or cocktails.

Laura has been featured in newspapers and on radio and TV, in addition to being on numerous podcasts and blogs.

She is the mother of ten, currently living in the Appalachians with her husband, their Irish Wolfhound Liadan, Bernese Mountain Dog Boo Bear, and their rabbits, sheeps, and chickens on Glenmirril Farm.

Www.lauravosika.com
www.glenmirrilfarms.wordpress.com

AFTERWORD

We hope you have enjoyed *Startled by MUSIC* and found some moments of joy within these pages!
At Gabriel's Horn, we offer a paying market to quality poets working in traditional forms. The *Startled by* series is an annual publication. We invite you to submit to our upcoming volumes:

2025   Children
2026   America
2027   Legend and Lore
2028   War and Peace
2029   Freedom
2030   Courage

These are subject to change, particularly if we receive enough submissions to put out two anthologies per year. Our most current information is at www.gabrielshornpress.com/poetry-anthology or contact gabrielshornpress@gmail.com

Index

Absher, J.S.

    At the Graves of Those Who Made Me Sing   28
    Between the Sets: Scenes from a Film Noir   9
    Decibels of Praise   58

Anderson, Jacqueline

    Christmas   61
    Crescendo   66

Caraveo, Vanessa

    A Child's Song   70
    Love Melody   72
    Marvelous Instrument   72
    Unforgettable Ballad   67

Cushing, Bill

    Hiromi's Imayo   40
    Imayo for Diana Schurr   38
    Imayo for the Soloist   47
    Ode to Otyken   41
    The Redbbone Pantoum   42

Fantod, Danny

    Jobe the One Man Band   50
    To the Stadium Where Pink Floyd Performed   36

Felio, Deb Y.

Homecoming	6
Nature	20

Gigliotti, C.M.

Three Haiku for Heinrich Schütz	39

Groch, Evie

Atonal Music in a Rondeau	19
Ode to Flamenco	32
Ode to Reiko, Our Hostess	30

Gurney, Jennifer

Charm	27
Cleaning	27
I see your breath	5
Mozart	38
Thunderstorm	17

Hardesty, Jerri

A Magical Moment	33
Casual Muse	46
Jesse	48
The Right Place at the Right Time	53
The Trashcan Man	49

Heathcote, Mark

 Composed Over a Lifetime   4
 Give Me a Link Between Music and Art   74
 God, He's the Greatest Conductor of Them All   63
 Irish Harps   73
 The Whisper of the Muse   60

Hope, Rebecca May

 Confidentiality   12
 Music Therapy   10
 Wreck   14

Isaac, Donna

 StreamingMusic   34

Lincoln, Christina

 Faith's Music   62

Maglas, Marieta

 Kyrielle for George Sand & Frédéric Chopin   43
 Pantoum for a Summer Dance   18
 Poem for a Love Song   3

Moore, Annette

 Music's Harmonies   69

Powell, C.R.

    Music and Beauty   2
    The Kazoo's Cry   8
    The Lilting Refrain of the Irish Sea   16

Reyes, Luisa

    The Best Set   26

Sachs, Roberta

    Bassoona   10
    Clarinet   11
    English Horn, Cor Anglaise   13
    Trombone   12

Sanders, Diana

    Blossom Symphony   22
    Electric   54
    Music   56

Sellers, J.A.

    Saxophone   75

Tekkan

    Uguisu   21
    Leaf in the Wind   68

www.ingramcontent.com/pod-product-compliance
Lightning Source LLC
Chambersburg PA
CBHW060846050426
42453CB00008B/855